God and the People
PRAYERS FOR A NEWER
NEW AWAKENING

GARY GUNDERSON

Publishing details

God and the People:
Prayers for a Newer New Awakening

© 2021 Gary R. Gunderson

ISBN 978-1-7324222-4-7

All profits from any sale of this book go to support
the educational work of Stakeholder Health.

For information contact Stakeholder Health at:
www.Stakeholderhealth.org
or on Twitter at @stakehealth

Cover design and DTP by J. R. Cochrane

Acknowledgements

A book of prayers comes from within, but in my case mostly from many years of formative and generative relationships. My parents prayed and meant it, but dad also said you could tell what a person believed by what committees they actually showed up at. He showed up at a lot. And mom showed me faith in action.

I also think of Dr. Wayne Merritt, my Greek professor at Emory and dear friend who gave me my introduction to Walter Rauschenbusch and taught me about the movement I didn't know had moved me. And Jimmy Carter and Bill Foege who quietly prayed as they publicly improved millions of lives. And the webs of Spirit and *poeisis* woven by Fred, Mimi, Arvind, Somava, Bobby, Alina, Terry, Dora, Heather, Heidi and Larry Pray. I am constantly lifted by the healing ways of my Wake Forest FaithHealth team.

I am oddly grateful for the weirdness of COVID that stopped my scurrying and forced me to be still. I thought with no small lament about the lives of my children and grandsons, Charles and Asa. My most simple prayers are for them.

Once again, I am humbled by the gifts and graces of TC, Jim Cochrane, Cagn Cochrane, Jerry Winslow and Tom Peterson who guided my earliest drafts toward more authenticity and through all the publishing complexities into your hands. And grateful for the brave Stakeholder Health webs of learning.

There is nothing less impressive than a writer writing. Thus, I'm grateful for the love and endurance of my wife and best colleague, TC.

Contents

Contents (cont.)

Foreword

Most prayers never become famous. There are except-ions, of course. The one taught by Jesus that asks for debts to be forgiven "as we forgive our debtors."[1] Or the one, often attributed to St. Francis, expressing the desire to become God's "instrument of peace."[2] In the last century, the Seren-ity Prayer, penned, prayed, and preached by Reinhold Niebuhr, became widely known.[3]

But of all the billions of prayers offered today in every human language, within the belief systems of many different religions (or no religion at all), it is entirely unlikely that any will become famous. Mostly, these everyday prayers will be simple, earnest expressions of the human spirit reaching for a connection to the sacred—to some mysterious, transcen-dent reality known to be greater than the one who is praying.

The prayers Gary Gunderson shares with us in this little book foster in anyone willing to enter fully into their spirit a sense of new possibilities for engagement with the sacred all around us in the communities where we live and serve.

These are prayers for action, not for armchairs. There are prayers here for families, for essential workers, for first responders, for scientists, and for healers. They are filled with hope and with vision. Above all, they abound in com-passion and in love. They awaken two kinds of wonder.

First, there is wonder at the goodness of the world created for us—astonished joy in the "leading causes of life," and amazement at life itself. Gunderson prays "Thank You for weaving in ways we could not know to hope. Give us pause to be grateful at the wonder."

We join in this wonderment when we read "Walnut, oak, sequoia and bristlecone taste your soil and call it good, rising up in praise to give shelter to the birds and playground for squirrels, each grateful in their life."

Like the ancient Psalmist, our author welcomes awe at the beauty and the bounty of life.

But there is another kind of wonder here—puzzlement over how things have gone dreadfully awry. How could we fail to join Gunderson in wondering about the unnecessary suffering of vulnerable people whose needs are unmet, often because of greed or insensitivity of those in power? Nor are such questions addressed vaguely to others who should know and do better.

The perplexing queries are addressed first to ourselves: "God, how have we come to this, so distant from each other and all the rich life flowing from You the Generous One?" If we hear in these prayers the voice of a poet, we also hear the words of a prophet calling for social justice, knowing for sure we should do better: "How do You stand it, God? What holds back your wrath and vengeance on all of us who care so little?"

So we find lamentations that jolt the conscience and also touch the heart:

The words ring false as tin,
Color off in light aslant,
How can I keep on singing
In this strange land?

In the end, however, the lament turns toward hope:

> That pain itself is witness to what
> > might be birth, yet.
> Come my father, mother,
> > sister, brother, friend.
> Come close now.

Gunderson knows that prayer can be questionable in a world like ours. Just how does one offer prayers for the whole public during a time of deep divisions, growing secularism, and remarkable religious pluralism? Our author does not address these prayers nebulously To Whom It May Concern.

These are not prayers to an impassive Force that might be with us. They are addressed to God—to one Gunderson calls You. Elsewhere, he refers to Maker God, Generous One, Surprising God, Ultimate One, and Weaver. It is evident throughout that these prayers are personal.

They are also richly social, intended for the "ragged gaggle called public." They are offered in the hope they might be useful to all the members of the beautiful quilt of a culture we call home, regardless of the religious labels we wear or reject. This is a book of prayers for all people of spirit.

But it is expressed in Gunderson's mother tongue, a language of somewhat uneasy faith, glimpses of which become clearer as we enter the book's final sections. He writes and prays, he says, "in tension with Jesus and those following in his Way."

The tension, it seems, largely results from the distance between ideals of the Way and our complicity in the realities of social injustice. So we pray not just for ourselves but for a society desperately in need of change.

Throughout this book there are many reasons for prayer, stated or implied. We pray to be emboldened, to seek clarity, to protect us from distractions, and "to be fully present to the world You are creating."

Of all the reasons, perhaps none is clearer than this: "We pray because the world is unfinished and we are still unfinished, our spirit still emerging and shaping."

Just so, let us pray.

Dr. Gerald Winslow
Loma Linda University

Chapter One

Before Praying

Praying

"Teach us to pray," they asked Jesus, expecting instructions. He disappointed and annoyed, as usual. But two thousand years later almost anyone attending a funeral can mumble along with the handful of phrases he offered.

We have also heard it in religious places by proper people with sonorous voices, so we miss it's radical simplicity. He spoke Aramaic in which the prayer was stark, with no temple polish at all. This is what he said, paraphrased from Matthew 6:7-13 (God save me):

> *"Mother, father, sister, brother and friend,*
> *Who makes everything sacred, and all life possible,*
> *we ask only enough for today.*
> *Release the burdens of yesterday as*
> *we release the debts of those we have burdened.*
> *Protect us from distraction and anything that is not of*
> *life.*
> *May it be."*

That's it.
That's all he said.
Doesn't seem like quite enough.

It wasn't his only prayer, of course. Most were even shorter. "Forgive them, they know not what they do." And, "Take this cup from me." Sometimes he just wept for what the city did not know.

He prayed most eloquently with his life, as spiritual people do, full of healing and groaning and weaving. The life resonated with intimate knowing of those he met on dusty paths and marble palaces. He told easily remembered, vivid stories that tended to mock the powerful and gave hope to those they thought beneath them.

He healed so many people in so many unauthorized ways that it drove those in politics and religious power to kill him. What kind of healing gets one killed? It starts with a simple, honest, humbling presence before the ultimate; prayer without the presence or performance. There grows an ember of something more disruptive than our schemes, programs and gizmos.

That kind of prayer opens space for clarity that untethers and propels. Who knows what happens next?

Praying is not the highest expression of spirit, just as writing is not the highest expression of thinking. Doing is where we integrate muscle and mind, sweat and spirit. But there is honor in word and voice as long as both serve; a cup of cold water or a visiting somebody in jail or the "good trouble" that gets one in jail.

You'll notice that I capitalize God and You, when I turn toward the ultimate. I'm showing respect, but do not presume chumminess. I know a 14 billion year continuing explosive phenomenon is not a buddy.

But the spirit breathing through it seems closer to a "You" than an "it." This book is not the one exploring the cosmological theology that difference implies. I'd like to read that book, but am not attempting to write it here. These are spiritual sketches, not hard-core systematic theology. I think it best to pray first.

Maybe we can pray together, you and me. I don't mean by you reading my words. I hope they trigger your own Spirit to find language from your life and labor. Maybe songs or images. The pages that follow have some of my prayers. Because I am careful with words, some of them look like poems, laid out on paper that you can scan with your eyes.

Voice would be much better; you could hear their tentative offering, my uncertainty seeking faith. They are sketches in spirit, which is why they are accompanied by sketches in pen by my friend Cagn Cochrane.

Better prayers are offered in sweat, not words. Spirit woven of broken threads into something new and useful for the world.

That kind of doing is a kind of thinking, sometimes even a kind of praying where words come long after. You'll find traces of that in these prayers typed and edited, but shared work would be better.

I hope we'll get to pray that way someday.
May that be.
May we become part of what is trying to become.
Protect us from distraction from anything that is not of life.

That's what I'm praying for.

Chapter Two

Cycle of the Day

Waking

Oh my God, a wholly new and unimagined day! What were You doing while we were resting? Surely the roots of billions of trees moved a bit further into the soil while trillions of flowers polished their colors. Winds and currents moved, lifting dew and bringing down the rain while we slept. Exactly what we needed! Molten rock beneath our sleeping bodies moving to shape new mountains for tomorrow.

So much is already under way. Bring us fully present to the world You are creating again and always.

We are small, but rested and ready for the tasks that fit our hands, the hopes from our beating hearts, the ideas we can grasp. You have washed our spirit clean and tuned our muscles and minds for this one and only day. Let us repay with the only thing You ask, our grateful attention.

Liberate us from our distracting aches and worries, the clutter of small annoyances. Rouse our spirit with the possibilities no longer hidden in yesterday.

Break us open and carry us into the beating heart of the world You so love.

Save us from grandiosity with laughter.

Look there at our toes! How strangely useful. Look there at our hands! How curiously formed to grasp the near edge of today. Look at these eyes, with wrinkles from all the other days still curious and open to today. Here is bread, milk, fruit and even coffee that others have made so we might be part of the waking of the whole world.

So many people You have
   brought near our own small life.

Let us see them with Your eyes and spirit,
   how they hurt in ways we might relieve,
   how they hope in ways we might nurture,
   what You might be giving us through
      them, if we would open ourselves.

Oh, for such a time as this, we are
   wonderfully made.

Making

Maker God, never ceasing lover of mercy, doer of justice, raiser of mountains. You move the seas and call forests from loam.

We are amazed that You call us to make, do and rise also. Hands and feet, not just voice. Not contained by yesterday. Always moving toward possibilities never seen before. Free, even to imagine and do mercy and justice.

Let us make the day with You.

Guide us like the tendrils of the forest roots and highest reaches branches growing toward life and light. Tune our ear to the cries of suffering and silenced hopes where You already are present.

Open our eyes to the powers and patterns that predict that suffering. Help us see where we are part of those patterns You despise. How to loosen the bonds by shifting our weight onto the side of justice, even if at a cost to ourselves.

Do not cast us away, but draw us onto the path of righteousness. Extend your mercy even unto us. Dare we ask that your mercy extend through us, too? Can even our lives be part of Yours, our hands Yours, our feet Yours?

Stir our hearts to be impatient for the waters of justice to roll quickly through dry channels and parched fields. Give us rest when we have earned it. But now let your energy flow through us and before us.

Let us taste your grace as liberty to be bold, generous and generative.

Make our muscles twitch for worthy work, fill our minds with questions worth asking and risks worth taking.

Water the soil with our sweat and gladden our toil with song from deep in the soul You have given us.

Make us bold. And bolden to make.

Quicken our steps with the confidence to leave the past and move toward You, your path and the work we are made to do.

May we be used entirely for the the life of the world.

We go in thanks.

Taking In

Generous One,

We are amazed by how much flows to and through us. Not one moment or a single step without others. We live on the food and fluid that brings us energy and mends out bodies. We are part of all who give us the stuff of life. We do not know who plowed and planted, harvested and transformed, packed, cooked and delivered to us so that we might live. Forgive us for how little we think of them as we eat, imagining our money is enough to claim the gifts given to us.

> As we taste the generosity
>> sharpen our appetite for mercy
>> till we are thirsty for justice.

You have made us wonderfully complex; inside, outside and in between. Cells beyond number, strengthening, replacing and healing so that no part of our body remains the same.

What is this thing called me? Is this thing called "us" less amazing? How are we bound with every particle fed and feeding?

> We are what flows through. Ever new and renewing, the Spirit moves us.

> Life we received, to strengthen choices serving life.

We taste the bread and savor the wine and delight in the flow to others. Made to eat and made to give. Then beckon us to the streets and the long journey.

Thank You.

Undone

Another day ends incomplete.

For those on the other side of our spinning globe, another day dawns. Here we lay down our bodies and tools. We are weary and feel the burden of all that is far from done. Our thoughts spinning still, even as our bodies slow.

Give us your blessing on our unfinished work. Some needs to be left behind, some is the seed for tomorrow.

You are never done, always redeeming the incomplete. Never ending, ever beginning, God.

Give us the peace to rest with the unfinished work of today.

Teach us to treasure the seeds yet to bear fruit, unfulfilled hopes yet to bloom.

Give us gratefulness for hopes too big for any one day, lifetime, family or tribe.

Thank You for muscles that need rest from the good ache of lifting with stamina for work they will not finish soon. For minds large enough to imagine things that need stillness to mature. For plans missing parts that draw us close to others. For partial clarity that needs others' eyes.

We thank You, for You are not done with us.

Show us the burdens that can be left behind.

Free us from wasted tenacity, merely for show.

Release all those who we imagine owe us something.

We rest knowing that many of those You love can never rest in day, dusk or dark for fear of violence, pain of hunger, the anxious stares of those they love. Help us see them and bring us close.

Give us grace as we accept your gift of stillness.

Touch our resting minds with images of your mercy extending through love of friends, good work of mercy, maybe even justice.

Just as we do not help the rains come, forests breathe and oceans swell, let us accept our limits as gifts of rest.

Now, let us rest deeply and well so that we might wake to the possibilities You are already working on.

Chapter Three

The Intimate Us

Always Blending God

You never quit stirring ingredients!

Thank You for mothers, fathers, sisters, brothers, cousins and the cloud of relationships beyond all vocabulary.

Thank You for energy that makes two one, then one three. Energy that fuses those of other mothers into families.

Energy that splits and blends again, replicating, multiplying, changing, moving, always new. Energy bringing and going, protecting, sending, teaching, forgetting, bruising, forgiving and forgiving again.

Even one cell of one body is too complex to grasp; how much more a thing called family.

Forgive our simple naming, the lines in our heads that trip us up and tie us down in real life. Forgive the expectations and projections with edges like knives. Dismiss the family of ghosts in our heads we hold more real than the actual humans in our lives.

Family is the kind-hearted surprise that shakes us and make us new again; the image of an ever-creating God. And family is our shame and pain where grief is buried and bitterness festers as we know not what we do. Release us and wash us clean of all distractions.

Family is how we give ourselves away as the stars have done for billions of ages to generate billions of planets—even our little one. Could we be generous for our handful of years in this little place, too? More kind and less correct, more hopeful and less needy, generous with less accounting, marked by the light we leave in motion.

Make us new now, for we are short-lived and must not tarry to be kind.

Amen

Daughters to Sisters

Thank You God who never ceases to generate new life from shared love, new love from shared life, never wasted, always creating and recreating.

Thank You for life woven from broken threads that a lesser god would waste.

Thank You for daughters and sons as they become sisters and brothers of their parents, teaching and tending us, as they once received.

What a delight to be held by those who love us. Our daughters and sons teach us so.

Thank You for weaving in ways we could not know to hope.

A hundred, thousand, million eddies in the current that deserve names and celebrations. Every one adding, rising up and laying down, old selves fallen away for the new.

As surely as the river flows You draw us, too, shaping the channel for those who come later. Teaching and releasing until gradually we are eye to eye. Then loved into memory, a story beyond us, as sons and daughters become memories themselves.

Thank You for weaving in ways we could not know to hope.

Give us pause to wonder. One parent and one daughter, one son and one brother are as galaxies in motion. Entire fields of relationship, dancing as waves in the dark.

You raise us to raise each other over and again.

Thank You for weaving in ways we could know to hope.

Give us the grace to release and shed the past

Just enough grace for the day we are in with those we are with.

Just enough vision of the life flowing through and among us.

Thank You for making us so woven in ways we could not know to hope.

Amen

Second Life Love

Ever-beginning God,

Love begins again, again. Still grateful for first life and fruits of family and the stuff of life that makes us. Less grateful for the blended pains of breaking, divergence, shards and pieces, bruises and loss never intended that makes us, too. Thank You that we can feel the pain that makes us alive and human.

Forgive the hurt we did not intend.

You always weave beginnings from endings. Heal by mending, sometimes blending in new ways. Let us never forget what you put together or take lightly what you have made now.

Turn our minds to that being born, among us and through us. You created us to be partners with You in giving birth to a child or four. Raised to be kind and grateful. And now,

another kind of possibilities for the life of the world to flow through. For every kind of birth, we give thanks to be present.

You have made us to delight to give ourselves away again and again. And shaped us to give life away, too. Where once we gave children caution and protection, tune us now for other births that need risk and unpredictability.

Give us the confidence You will protect us enough for the journey, food enough to travel light and quickly to where You need us. With shelter and care enough to travel low to the ground. Light enough to see the next steps; courage enough to take them.

Give us love in this second life; for each other and the journey. Free us from taking ourselves too seriously. Come music, voice, drink, dance, rest, poems, laughter and play along the way.

For the world spins in love and love is good.

We are amazed!

Chapter Four

Social Body

Shredded

Broken God; rejected, scorned, despised, mocked and misunderstood by the cruel. You have made us for kindness, to hope for and help each other. We see the generous possibilities. But we are easily bruised, disappointed; vulnerable at exactly the places we turn for strength.

We do not understand how we have come to be so shredded and separated from those we depend on for the most basic flow of food, water and stuff from which we craft our lives. How have we come to be this way? And how do we find ourselves again?

We find our capacity to care shrinking into smaller and smaller circles; just me and a few of mine. Right now, here, what I want next. Me, now, here. Diminished, contained and afraid.

So we seek the tribe, Us, now, here. Defined by who we are not. Accusing You of making a world too small, needing fracture and competition for every scrap of every kind.

Your fault, God, the awful joke of kindness.

Against your human family and against all of life. We, diminished to grabbing and holding, wrapped in plastic, chattering and rushing, powered by the fumes of ancient life. Baking our tasteless gruel; whining for more.

God, how have we come to this? Distant from each other and all the rich life flowing from You, the Generous One? How do we find ourselves again?

Proud, but not without prophets and poets. Lost, but not without teachers and playwrights. Dull, but surrounded by birdsong, bees and forests. Dry, but still comes the dew and the tides.

It may be too late and our best too small.

But maybe not.

Break open our hard hearts till broken edges find each others'. May our silence call out another's voice. May our dullness awaken through another's prayer.

Maybe.

May it be.

Who Loves the Whole

God who loves every little bit of every little thing
Of the ragged gaggle called public,
Light our way with what both You and science see as sacred, blessed, honorable, worthy of praise and sacrifice.

Thank You for the amazing array of practices, behaviors, choices that lead to life; that protect, enhance, extend and spread its blessings widely across the people.

Stop us from holding on to ourselves anything that You intend for "all."

We see that You are not done because we can see science is not done.

Every day You reveal new possibilities worth doing together, as we can see how your science is a friend of humans, and shows how much mercy and justice is possible.

Never let your public health servants stop talking about facts, analytics, determinants, vectors, patterns and predictors. Nurture their crazy love for the people—the public.

Feed our hope for better, more and broader health. Even when those with smaller hopes take our money, or put us in the dumpy offices, and cut our staff. Even when those afraid of your vision treat us badly.

Do not let us quit.

Keep us in our lovers quarrel with the public.

Protect us from those who have lost their love for the public. Release them to them less consequential work not played for life and death stakes. Move them someplace they will not endanger the people.

Do not make us proud of our righteousness, but give us delight in being part of those who just can't stop loving your messy, disappointing, ever-muddling humans called "the public."

Thank You for placing us in JUST the right work at just the right time.

But never let us speak out of pride; Love first, last, and in between; especially in public, especially with the public, especially about the people You so love.

Between Clarities

Ever unfolding One,

We live between clarities about the most important things. It makes it hard to pray. We are not clear if You invented us to have someone to talk to or if we invented You for the same reason.

Perhaps You have second thoughts, too, always rising up a mountain, then changing your mind and raising up an ocean instead. Ages of changing your mind about entire species. Perhaps this is how we are in your image.

Embrace our disbelief as a kind of respect for what is still moving.

How can our little intellects imagine a larger one, more creative, patient, kind and nuanced? How does one imagine without hands? How would one lament without the limitations of a short and painful life? How would one hope, while knowing every painful failure, the banal brutality of race, the struggle ahead of the children?

We sense in our bones the universe is home. But our lives are too short for the slow cadence of wisdom. We are such a short-lived species to take in such wonder.

We hardly know the fantastic complexity in the soil on which we walk, the slow witness of the forest through which we move. Our thoughts are less sensitive than any tendril of any root.

How can we grasp the bent and twisted cry of the ancient, but still-folding stone, speaking of ceaseless change? We feel the rain but overlook its kiss; feel the breeze but fail to notice the caress.

We see the new sun, but hardly notice the promise of energy beyond measure. We notice the sun going down but miss the benediction. A thousand gifts a day from a universe made as home; and we plod through unexcited.

Let us be quiet together, show respect by silence instead of chatter. Look together from soil to stars, microbes to brothers, sisters, mothers and children? Give us peace in silence. And welcome the embrace.

May it be.

Children Old Too Soon

God on the run, born of parents who ran to safety when the soldiers came. Fled the garage when the shepherds left and and crossed the desert wastes to give your life a chance.

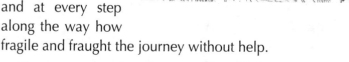

Your mother without a husband, your father without a story, refugees against an empire.

You knew early and at every step along the way how fragile and fraught the journey without help.

You must weep for others even less likely to find one.

Be with the children on their own.

They listen in the silence for the next blow to fall.

Listen for the cold weight of anger from one supposed to protect, they wait for the punch on the way.

Listen for the scurry of the vermin and the scatter in the dark. Listen for the parent who is working instead of tending.

Listen to the names of shame and stigma.

Listen for someone to say their name in kindness.

They are watching for a crack and the slight light. Watch and read the flow of the day and what might come next.

Watch for kind eyes and an open hand. Watch for something to eat and drink. Watch for a safe place to wash.

Child God, the human one, bring us to the children on their own. May we listen and watch for them. You know their lives; teach us as would be with them. Each child a savior of us all.

Give us eyes to see the child old too soon.

And eyes for pattern of the ten, hundred, thousand and million as clear as one child's cry.

Strengthen our hearts and sharpen our eyes to see the utterly predictable processes and places bereft of justice, even the shreds of mercy.

How do You stand it, God? What holds back your wrath and vengeance on all of us who care so little?

Tear away the hiding place from the ugly shadow of our lazy charity, of kindness held small.

Give us no mercy and make us fear justice.

As a child, come to us and wake us up.

Those Who Pray For Others

Beaten down God;
thrown from synagogues,
killed for grace
and liberation
by the easy complicity of priest and power.

Give those who think they speak for You
Pause.
Mindless to the moment already sacred.
Pause.
Before speaking of others' pain.
Or emptiness.
Or loneliness.
Or hope, too tender for words.
Pause.
For those of us who speak unrepented,
Our second, third and twentieth coat hanging in
    in the closet
        asking You to warm a stranger,
        a child of yours.
Pause.
Until we come as a child.
A bee longing for the hive.
An acorn pressing the first tendril into the soil.
An old man hoping yet to be of use.
Then tenderly

Catching the scent of grace
and Presence
Remembering silences true.
Come as to a father, mother, sister, son, brother,
Come deep and wide as the rushing stars as
All of everything says yes, I am;
Be home in Your home.
Rest now.
Even me.
Even us.

Good Trouble

God of anger, fire, trouble and cry.

Kindle us, your willing embers of the world that needs a cleansing fire.

We are yours to risk, eager for fresh air beyond the safe spaces.

We love your street, and concrete grit. We love the stride and the heft of things worth doing, unafraid of conflict.

Let us not hold your energy lightly, unexamined and unwashed of pride. Let us not waste your hope by tethering it to our short-ranging vision. Let us not waste voice and language by limiting it to our cleverness.

Tune our ears to those hardest to hear, the ones we find annoying and inconvenient. Especially help us hear the ones that embarrass our proper friends, just as You bothered them with tax collectors, working women and the rich.

You were rejected by family, nearly thrown off a cliff by neighbors. Complicate our sense of connection and draw us into the tangled humanity You have made so wonderfully and inconveniently complex.

And then, after we sense the breadth of your impossibly wide family, let us speak with simplicity of mercy and justice in kindhearted firmness.

Protect us last. Put our bodies in the way of those who would harm the poor and despised; let the bruises intended for the weak fall on us; let the venom aimed at the despised be ours. Spend us as You have spent yourself.

We know in resistance we find release; in giving, all gain. For life finds a way where we let it flow through us into lives parched for mercy, aching for justice, despairing of peace. May our young be brave. Our families raising up new prophets as our old ones take the risks reserved for those who have lived enough to give it all away.

Make our lives a protest against the lie that You have not created enough food, space and freedom to go around for all your children. We deny with generous lives the lie that You failed to design a world that might work for us all.

May our kind lives protest the lie that we must narrow our hope to only those who pray like us, look like us and talk like us.

May our lack of anxiety protest the bitter penury that shrinks your mercy into a fist.

Surely it is your voice that speaks of a time when your promises will be realized, the weapons laid down, the rich with the poor eating together, lamb and honeybee, Baptist and Buddhist, Anglican and Atheist quiet in wonder at how great Thou art, how blessed we are.

May it be.

Keep Trying

God who never quits
Picking up the pieces of
A day in disarray;
Early light showing the damage,
Of more than one bad night;
A thousand choices poorly made,
Ten thousand choices not made at all
That could have helped.

We grieve what could have been.
While You begin again.

God of broken threads
Weave again, mending.
God of broken hopes,
Weave again, blending.
Even limping, let us be woven
blending
In the current of another day
Not ending
yet.

Who are we to quit,
If You keep healing?
Who are we to rest,
If You keep on?

Replace our hopes of pride
with work enough for the day—
Enough steps on the way.
Grace, if not peace,
Peace, if not rest.

Feed our hunger for mercy,
Make us thirst for justice.
Sharpen our ache for what is not yet here,
All energy and spirit beneath
What comes next,
The substance of that not seen,
More than memory,
Still possible.
Try again.

Chapter Five

Essential Workers

Essentials

Patient, diligent One.

We offer our lives of service.

We are the ones who carry the mail, inspect the food, visit the home bound, carry the wounded, answer the phone for the cry for help, or just the cry.

We are the ones who figure out the city, county and schools, finding a way, making all the mundane decisions for not much thanks.

We tend the wires, pave the roads, trim the trees, repair the bridges, pick up the trash and ones left behind.

We love the bad things that did not happen, in the wounds avoided or at least not left to fester. We like fires averted. And small bruises healed.

We awake knowing we cannot do all that calls out for us before sleeping.

We cannot make the garment whole.

We cannot hope to rest, if rest comes only when the work is done.

Give us peace in seasons of sorrow and frustration, as we know too many undone mercies, and out-of-reach justice. We have such little reach; give us patience for our part of the unfolding and peace in the labor we can grasp.

You know how it feels to be "essential" for decades unthanked.

We lose our way and doubt the value of our lives. May we sense your unfolding and emergent action beneath us and before us? Can You give some taste of the mercy we thirst for, a slender scent of justice that might feed us in the wilderness of a hard-hearted time?

What in your universe is not essential? We are humbled by the slow weaving of possibilities from the stone and wind worn into beauty as it gives soil to bear fruit and honey. Our lives as brief and narrow, like one root in a forest, one flap of a wing on a great journey we will not finish.

Give us your peace to savor the work within our grasp, the kindnesses we can pass along.

You work without ceasing, so we pause without finishing this prayer, sensing even as we ask, Yes.

Responding First

God who never leaves the wounded behind
Who never gives up on what others' discard,
Be kind to those who do the same.

First Responders often respond alone
When the overdose finds its way into a life degraded.
When the desperate one falls even further
Striking out at themselves or someone near.

We will look away
Only when you look away.
Never look away.
Keep our eyes open wide
But protect our heart.

The uniform hides a life
Worn beyond words,
Unexplained, misunderstood by family and faith.
Often alone for weary hours, exposure, cold and shock.
Wounds unhealed and not forgotten.

Ever-responding God, how do You do it again every day?
As if yesterday's loss did not predict today's?
Do You ever feel trapped by what others did not do?
You do not forget the lost,
nor what is yet possible.
Even without justice, there might be mercy.
May it be enough for now.

Give us mercy in our own bones,

The weary ones.
Give us mercy in our mind,
The weary one that knows too much to rest easily.

Give us comfort in those you send prisoners of hope like
    us.
That should we call, they will respond.
That should we fall behind, they will not be slow to
    notice.
That our wounds are not beyond reach either.

May we find some mercy now.

Collecting

God of the discarded,
  left behind and unwanted.
Bless those who gather the lost, unloved, unnecessary
  and wasted.
Who lives more like You than they?
Who rises early to tend to what others leave
  thoughtlessly?
Who labors in nameless humility at work no one else
  would do?

Who faces the dawn, the cold, the rain, wind exposed?
Who accepts disdain that makes even one's bones cry
out?

Disturb we who waste.
Our unreflected appetite flows onto the streets
and into trucks that feed the burial mounds.
Forgive, but awaken.
Awake as You, to the world of those on whom their life
depends.
Awake as You, to the trash that is still theirs, still rests to
their account.
We are not worthy of your love or their service.
Forgive us for your love wasted, your creation
disrespected.

Comfort those most like You
Who pick up what others leave behind
Meeting thoughtlessness with diligence and duty.

Give them strength for the day and
Honor from essential work done well.
May their children bless them for what they do.
May their church revere them for their witness to your
ever-patient mercy
Risking your own to give to others the very chance at life.

Weaving and Connecting

God who is everywhere all of the time,

Help us who often feel alone, distracted and disconnected.

God who makes the planets spin, oceans move, and mountains rise,

Help us who feel caught and fraught.

God who made muscles and bone, and pulls blood through our veins to every cell in our body,

We fear You have not made us strong enough for the burdens of those You have brought into our lives. Forgive us our fear so your life can flow to every person in your body.

We pray to connect and support.

Weak, small and limited as we are,

We dare to ask that You connect us and support those who need the most basic evidence of your love. Move us to where your love is extended, but lacks the kind voice, the food You want them to have, the electricity You want in the wires of their home, the heat You wish for them to feel against the cold, the guidance they may not be able to hear directly from your Spirit.

We dare to ask that You translate your boundless love into immediate, tangible practicalities, relevant and real against the fears and anxiety one of your children is experiencing. We ask your energy to bring us into relationship with those You already love. We ask You to use us to interpret your love into the words, action and things they might experience as your healing.

The systems are complex beyond our grasp. Free us from trying to be You, the Weaver. Use us as your thread, broken and frayed, but adequate for You to weave a fabric for someone.

You, the artist and the needle; we the thread glad to be pulled into your design.

God, You have shown us the day beyond time when we are joined only and purely by your spirit. With that confidence, give us energy enough for this one day.

Knowing how our race will end, give us now vision enough for the next right steps, the handful of tasks that fit our hands to express your grace and love on this one day.

You have put the same prayer in the hearts of all those necessary to accomplish your loving kindness. Give us peace in our small part.

We see that our bones and muscles are worthy, that nothing that flows through is ever wasted.

In being used and given away, we are not only enough, but complete, at least for this one day.

Thank You for the breath coming into and through our every cell, alive in your love, connected and whole.

Artists

Pigment, pixel,
Charcoal, chisel,
Paper, canvas,
Sketches in sand,
Or on the web,
Word, line or note,
Offered up from
the wonder
beyond us.
Let us not weary of trying.
Hold tender this yearning
    to strip away distraction,
    to notice the tone more true.
Craft our courage to craft,
Draw our skill and diligence closer,
    closer to the soil.
Like the tendril easing from the
    acorn into the dark moistness
Awaken us to savor the soil of a new
    thought,
Lament when the sorrow moves,
Wonder at emergence,
Delight when tone rings clear,
Savor elements well served.

It is good to be here,
Present, alive. Alert.

Skeptics

Why and why not?
How and how not?
If and if not?

God bless those who question, ponder and
    question again;
Testing every thought and every test, too.
We call it science, but fundamental to wonder.
As hopeful and tentative as any saint.
Just as any pilgrim is skeptical of those who
    think themselves complete,

God bless the scientist.
Protect their sacred skepticism of anything
    through too sacred to question.
Protect their tender vein of curiosity from all
    the things they are proud to not believe.
Hold safe like a young sprout in Spring
The thoughts and questions just emerging, a
    thought seeking mind like a seed does soil.

God bless the scientist
Guard their heart as they pass through the
    certain things—
frailty, dependence, loss of love,
voice and sight, the steady hand,
quick mind,
regard of friends
confidence of worth,
all pass like dust.

Ground in wonder
  at every breath taken
  at every thought considered.

Test against the world they so respect
  as You so love,
  amid, not apart,
    worth revealing as another beginning.

Slow yes

God who says yes to life
And no to death;
Yes to the ways that lead to life
And no to those that separate.
Yes to hope
No to helplessness,
No to fear.

So easy to see the unclaimed yes in others;
How can they say no to obvious gifts?
So hard to see our own choices waiting
    like clean air to breath in.
Why do we hold our breath?

We pray for the slow yes.
The vaccine untaken, though others risk
    everything to offer it freely.
The vote uncast, though others faced down
    dogs and bullies to make it possible.
The careless waste, as the planet melts in
    plain sight.
The kindness waiting.

Do not give up on us.
Stir in us the seed of yes.

You made us for life,
    life as one people;
People in one common life.
Yes. Yes. And Yes again.

Healers

God, we pause to mind the healers with beepers and phones vibrating with urgencies stretching into the long hours ahead of every day.

Just as they know how to avoid giving the wrong drug, protect us from raising up a false prayer for their brilliant tenderness. How different they are, like the cells of the body they protect.

You stir the healing heart of every race, politics, legal status, gender, education, professional role and faith.

Take away our spirit mask and distance so we can be infected by your ever spreading love.

Unlike a virus, which spreads without thinking, give us eyes and hearts wide open to every opportunity to heal with purpose and make others strong. But do not pass us by, for we, your hands of healing, need healing, too. We know too much of the frailties. Our families are scared for us, too.

So, bring us near. Close enough to know that trust and generosity are never wasted.

You have made us for these days and to be among thousands of other healers.

Use us.

Thank You.

Chapter Six

Passages

Moving

Creator, evolver, God,

Made to move, and we do. Made to notice, too. Forgive how much we miss by hurrying past. Forgive us for moving without seeing.

Even one human pace crosses a universe evolved. How can we be so oblivious? Far beneath us the folded, lifted and long-traveled stone still moves. Why are we not more amazed? No cathedral more crafted; yet we stride past unmoved. The ridge that was an ocean, the ocean that was molten. You raise us up, too and carve over eons. Why do we not laugh out loud at the absurd generosity?

Could You raise us up, too? Carve away our pride, mold our molten Spirit?

The loam above the rock, each inch of leaf-fall, an offering of a trillion of your tiny servants. Walnut, oak, sequoia and bristlecone taste your soil and call it good, rising up in praise to give shelter to the birds and playground for squir-

rels, each grateful in their life. Could You bring us home, too? Could we find home where You have planted us?

Who could miss the rainbow, watercolors in the moist sky? We may not notice You do the same in rock, rainbows of color laid down across millions of years, painted with wind blown sand, then countless trillions of creatures, pigment clay washed from hundreds of miles; red, ivory, brown, green, impossible blue and carbon black. Could we appreciate our layered lives, too? Have patience to love what comes and what goes?

Everywhere we think too cold and dark, You live. Beneath the sea, even into the rock, your life finds a way. The furthest reach of galaxies, a pulse and stuff of life. Painted caves of wonder, love and family, hopefulness and loss. You have made this all our home, if only we would be here.

We do not pray for changeless safety, but to be fully present and awake to the pulse and pace. Forgive us the wasted fuel, time and frenzy to hurry somewhere else. Slow us down, caught by the wonders we might miss; the traveling mercy of noticing where we are.

Viaticum

Ever-beginning, always-ending God,

We thank You for both endings and beginnings and ask
for help with the anxieties both produce.

There are rituals that help us approach the end of life,

And beginnings of marriage,

The birth and consecration of a child.

Help us not pass lightly the recovery from illness and
return to a life changed, and not quite the same.

How do we mark the sacred ending of marriage so that
life continues healed for those that loved and still care.

So many passages unmarked, the constant new births in
any human life,
the tectonic pressures and liberations that happen in
between the named events;

when we see ourselves with new eyes as
old expectations finding new hopes.

Passage from teacher to learner, friend to partner,
colleague back to friend,
partner to lover,
caregiver to receiver and back again until the life is
a garment mended with borrowed thread.

Grant us liberations of endings and beginnings,
inflections and discontinuities
missed by holding tightly, thinking that only now is
sacred.

Sacred is the flow that carries us as surely
as the bird on the wind,
the mountain on the magna
the fish in the sea.

Plenty for the journey.

Those in Silence

Weeping God of sorrows,
Come tenderly to those who know sadness in these
 days,
The aching grey hours before dawn, when You
 wept for the city.
And the heart-bound vacancy at noon.
The loneliness of overheard laughter,
The touch observed, meant for someone else.

Words ring false as tin,
Color off in light aslant.
How can I keep on singing
In this strange land?

Hold me now and gather me close.
Even now my heart beats.
Even now, my blood moves in my veins.
Even now, my muscles ripple for weight to lift and
    work to do.
Even now, draw me toward those even more alone.

God of sorrow, testify that pain is life unfinished yet,
That unresolved sadness may yet focus on what is
    not yet done,
  witness to what might be birth.
  Come my father, mother, sister, brother,
  friend.
  Come close now.

Lament

Forests turned to dust and
    trinkets,
Tundra melted for plastic,
prairie paved.
We lament
For what we have done
And left for others to repair.

For what we have taken on
    our behalf.

For those we have wounded
    or for
pain inflicted on those we did
    not know, on our behalf
cascade of violence designed to leave us undisturbed,
Grazing like cattle on the innocent.

For birdsong we no longer hear amid the distraction.
For the creaking of the tall trees in the wind, we no
    longer notice.
For the water flowing clean and cold, we no longer
    taste.

Sharpen our pain for what is lost and
lost beyond reach.
Gone a thousand years, ten times more
beyond return.
For the generations who will never
know what was.
Lament.

The pain testifies that we are not done,
Witness to beauty defiled but not
beyond redemption.
To mercy lost, but not yet without
healing.
To justice desecrated, but not yet
absent hope.

May new conviction spring up from
bitterness of loss
Nurtured by energy of ever emergent life
That will not give up on the world God loves,
That will not give up on the people God loves,
Given freely
Released completely to what might yet be.

Garage Baby

Amazing you ever made it out of the garage. Dangerous and disruptive from the first breath. Dodging power from the first rumor; then covered in tinsel, bluster and pomp ever since. Your mom and dad, canny to flee the slaughter. And brave enough to set You loose among the little priests and politicians who predictably killed You.

Preposterous Savior. Help our unbelief.

Give us a slender tether to your promise of the end of power, end of religion; end of all that sad and gloomy weight of one over another—we lesser ones owing the greater ones.

No more freedom paid in blood, guilt and supplication.

The end of all that.

The end of all that.

Do not be afraid, say the angels.

Unless You have money, religion or law; then be very afraid. Lay down another liberation.

No wonder, then, the slaughter of the babies, seed of such dangerous hope.

Feed our slender hope of entering the womb again.

Jesus' Prayer

Mother, father, sister, brother and friend,

Who makes everything sacred, and all life possible,
we ask only enough for today.

Release the burdens of yesterday as we release the debts
of those we have burdened.

Protect us from distraction and anything that is not of
life.

May it be.

(Adapted from The Lord's Prayer, Matthew 6:7-13)

Writer's Prayer

Too many words;
From typing before thinking,
Thinking before noticing
Noticing without reverence
Forgive, again.

Thank You for the hunger to hold meaning
And thirst that testifies
We are not lost
or random,
alone
or mute.

Thank You when the right word comes.

Release my pride
As life edits.

Chapter Seven

After Prayer

A Newer New Spirit

By the time you've turned enough pages to get to this one, I hope you've been writing your own prayers in your one and only voice. That's the point. These next pages may help you think about that process, which may not be the best way to actually get there. Prayer is better done than thought about.

But thinking about praying in the early part of the 21st century does take some explanation. Some of us are out of practice; others disgusted by those whose prayers seem to make them mean. Prayer itself is part of how we do the labor of life, and we have a lot of work to do for our melting planet.

Three questions deserve some attention before I let you go. First, what can we learn from earlier movements of great awakening? Second, who or what is listening when we pray? Finally, what does Jesus have to do with any of this?

This last question may be particular to the tribe following after Him, of which I am a part. I see a new movement of Spirit that undermines all of our labels, including the ones that sort us into different theological camps, as well as those who don't want a Theo in their Ology. Our times are so radically fluid and unformed that it is hard to trust the words of anyone who believes their words adequate. Premature clarity smothers the most interesting, if not troubling, aspects of life.

I'm a Baptist influenced by Baha'i, Buddhist, Druid, Native American, African and Muslim Spirit as I've experienced it from those sharing their work and life. I still generally go to church, not rotating among the list. But I've learned that one doesn't need to agree on very much to pray together. Dr Jerry Winslow notes that most any thinking Christian in the 21st century is probably participating in some blend that would in earlier days be considered heresy. "I'm not sure my heresy has a name." If I were Muslim or Bhuddist I would need to locate myself there, probably with a heresy more suited to a different part of the spiritual spectrum.

Feel free to skip any or all of these questions.

A Newer New Awakening

We are obviously beyond many of the defining characteristics of our industrial civilization: post-modern, post-Christendom, post-Constitutional order. It is not at all clear what we are beginning, but I believe that the scaffolding and eventually sustained structure of civilization emerges out of its Spirit.

While theology is often written after the cement has dried, Spirit is part of the disruptive and reconstructive process around which institutions later find form. This is why times of radical change are often marked by upwelling of new forms of Spirit, as has been the case in each of the major transformations in the United States.

One of those phase changes was marked by Rauschenbusch and his prayers; they are obviously my prompt.

We are beginning. Again. In every Beginning and every beginning since, was the image, the imagination, the Spirit of curiosity about what might emerge. This is true in different ways all around the world wherever humans find themselves maladjusted to the way things are, needing another Beginning. The anti-slavery movement globally—and in the USA—was protected with religiosity and then destroyed with untethered Spirit, expressed in astonishing acts of creative courage over many decades. Dr. King once observed that well-adjusted people never changed anything. The Spirit makes one maladjusted to standard brand reality.

These prayers and this book trace to a sermon I gave many years ago: "God is not done." It had many clever turns of phrase that were probably too clever, so my friend and professor, Wayne Merritt, came over afterward, handed me three books by Rauschenbusch, and gave some advice. He told me not to go anywhere near a pulpit without reading that great but flawed voice of the "new spirituality" of the Social Gospel. Ever since, I have prowled used bookstores for hundred-year-old copies of his books, especially the incendiary prayers. We need *newer* new ones.

Who was Walter and what does his work teach us these decades later? He was a thoughtful German Baptist pastor who finished his theological training and marched with confidence into a neighborhood of Hell's Kitchen in New York. He found immigrants crushed together, used and broken by the banal and anonymous cruelty of industrializing America. There was no glove on the corporate fists that beat down the poor and dispensable. His seminary tools were entirely irrelevant.

He fled to Berlin to study what this Jesus fellow was actually about. Could that long-ago life offer any clues at all how to live amid such naked and brutal suffering? He discovered an itinerant preacher who despised religiosity as

he talked to the insignificant, oppressed and occupied people. The priests, academics and politicians resented him, and eventually conspired to kill him. What did he talk about?

He spoke recklessly about God's *unfulfilled* hopes for people living in the social and economic realities that violated everything a God of mercy and justice wanted. The *social reality* was where the Good News was happening.

Of course, while Jesus *embodied* that radical hope, he didn't make it up. He learned it from the great prophets of the Jewish people. And he wasn't the last who dared, risked clarity and lived courage. It is impossible not to notice the resonance between Jesus, Mohammed, Buddha, Gandhi, King, Mandela, Lewis—of their hopes and the fears of those who eventually fought them.

This Social Good News of the early 1900's blew apart stale religious containers and set loose energy flowing into the streets and working places where people lived together. It dared to look for God in the life we are alive in *now*—not just the next life. It found the sweat of mercy more sacred than the razzle dazzle after death. It was the end of religiosity and it devalued religious pomp to near irrelevance.

Pastor Rauschenbusch and thousands of other like him didn't just pray. Their awakened Spirit made them bold in very practical ways. They created a vast and intricate array of emergent social structures. Their movement flowed into the body politic, which in many cities made possible public health departments. The social spirit movement created much of the non-profit sector of modern society that we know today, including food banks, social services, hundreds of hospitals, thousands of units of housing, and ministries, beyond all counting.

Most of that stuff is still here a century later. If you took all of that tangible evidence of Spirit out of any American city, you would hardly recognize the bleak and dismal landscape that would be left.

The movement was wrong, to be sure, about almost as much as it got right. And its leaders ignored as much as they saw. "*King*-dom" language excluded women right off the bat, which happened at the exact moment women were fighting and winning the right to Vote. The omission was not accidental; they were wrong on purpose because they decided that full justice was just too much to try for. Rauschenbusch had daughters and still got this wrong!

Still staggering out of the debris of the post-Civil War, the movement almost entirely denied the claims of Black Christians who knew the very most about Spirit and com-passion. Again, this wasn't ignorance; it was a political choice. The movement was amazingly naïve about how political and economic elites so easily capture religious energy for their own purposes.

Rauschenbusch also wrote of "Christianizing America," which makes 21st Century hair stand on end. And then catch fire. Religious language can warm the house and burn it— the Capitol, too, as we've seen.

But there was a time when Gospel language served just and inclusive policies. The spirit movement lent energy to politics that created fundamental policies such as those that enabled faith-based hospitals by the hundreds, public health departments, unions, child labor laws and restraints on the robber barons.

This movement of social good news was fiercely opposed by religious groups that called themselves "conservative." As now, those "conservatives" were actually quite radical in their theological innovations that downplayed Jesus's own life in favor of an abstraction called "Christ." They invented entire logic systems to escape the world that God created. It is as if they—and the current heirs to their thinking—were afraid of the world God so loved. If the Social Gospel movement was deeply flawed, at least it loved the world God made.

The Social Gospel movement was unattractively proud of itself, which made for easy capture by politicians willing to ride along with the convenient parts of the agenda, while ignoring the parts against war or for justice. The main beneficiary of social gospel politics, Woodrow Wilson, led the United States into the trenches of Verdun. Afterward he was complicit in the the ugly colonial appropriation of Africa and Asia that we are still digging out of a century later.

Rauschenbusch was a good enough man to die depressed, aware of the long shadow of his flaws and complicities. He knew his movement had easily succumbed to war fever and other varieties of cynicism. It was easily stigmatized by even prouder people such as Reinhold Niebuhr who loved "realism" as much as he did idealism. Walter's daughter, to his great annoyance, was *more* progressive than he. She poignantly saw his failure. Yet with a daughter's heart and longer vision, she counted his labor great because she knew it was unfinished but alive.

Movements have lives far beyond their leaders in unpredictable ways. Another Baptist Pastor named Martin attended the same seminary where Rauschenbusch taught. A Black man, less tempted toward triumphalism, King hoped only to *bend* the arc of history toward justice. He accomplished that, but died in Memphis, leaving much for another movement to complete.

Painful experience teaches us to keep religion and politics as far apart as possible. But that turns out to be not very far. We can't keep them entirely detached without ceasing to be human, *especially* at social, cultural and thus political level. There is little safety in imaginary separation.

Safety lies in nurturing a Spirit that is good for the world that the God of mercy and justice loves. Both science and constitutional law depend on faith and the ferment of hope it generates. Both depend on the consciousness that wisdom and science are not complete, *yet*. And that a democratic people can aspire for more mercy, justice and well-being than we have yet attained.

That stirring for more is not just the plodding extension of rationality, but something moral and Spirited because we are alive, conscious and spirited: *Homo sapiens sanctus*.

That earlier movement warns, but also invites, us to the work of Spirit. The tools of science and Spirit are both dangerous without moral vision for the good of all people. Both can be tuned to serve the tribe against others. And both can draw us forward toward more mercy and justice.

God is Still Not Done

We have wasted so much time. As a young parent, I remember being deeply worried about the shredded nature of the world in which my daughters would live. Now they have children and even more chilling evidence of the broken social and environmental systems.

We have learned so much about the patterns that undermine and exhaust even the superabundance of the created Earth. Every few weeks another group of scientists tries to cast another apocalyptic vision of doom which falls unheard by the next new cycle.

Perhaps we are too late even for the God who loved it all into being. But maybe not. Maybe the relationship of human and Ultimate is not delusional.

Maybe God is still not done.

Between Clarities

There is nothing like a global pandemic and eco-logical meltdown to call out a new Spirit. The earlier movements I've cited were overwhelmingly Christian, at least in the public.

It was never that simple. Obviously, from the earliest landing/invasion onto these shores the Spirit/politics/culture of the First People shaped the interplay with those coming from Europe on ships, funded by pilgrims and British invest-ors. The extraordinary resilience of the African Spirit en-abled the survival of the middle passage, slavery, and its reconstructed variations even unto today. Jewish, Muslim, Asian and Indian Spirit have long swirled into entirely un-namable currents producing complex political and social innovations.

We are in a whole new soup today: Post-Christendom, post-postmodern, post-industrial, post-oil, post-sexual cla-rity, post-Constitution and, thankfully, post guru. What are we becoming? What kind of News would be Good for our new social reality?

Sometimes we have a chance to pray in my very favorite place, the daily "safety huddle," where someone from every single operating unit of the hospital gathers to almost military protocol to make sure everyone is collaborating around the "events, concerns and needs" that might affect the lives of the patients and staff. We look away from our machines and screens to make eye contact with the other humans sharing the tasks of healing.

It is as practical as humans can get. Until COVID-19, the chaplains were contained to a Monday innovation, but the physicians asked for more, so now every morning ends in prayer.

These are people who are utterly committed to doing mercy and justice with their every waking hour, but mostly do not have any inclination toward religion, ritual or theology. If forced to commit to anything beyond the next urgent task, most would say they believe in science.

I love to pray with these people who rarely think about prayer at all. They are usually not at all clear what exactly is happening when one prays, nor do they feel it necessary to think about it. They are happy with two simple standards: No pretend prayers; and make sure that anyone listening knows it is for them, no matter their race, politics, legal status, gender, education, professional role or faith.

That's all the clarity we need. So the prayers in this book are for you, too.

Spirit as Civic Muscle

The multiple over-lapping crises of our time have broken us to our knees, even unto prayer. Many visions have emerged from panels of experts suggesting how we could turn around and then move forward. No small number of panels are driven by our advanced ecological catastrophe, and the reservoir of ideas about what we could do.

And now comes COVID-19 wielding destruction, disruption and the fire of illumination about how many of our social realities are interlocked. The bad news of our social vulnerabilities cries out for some good news of a profound nature.

A recent work called Springboard emerged out of the COVID-19 epidemic. It imagined a reweaving of many facets of our social fabric, some of which trace their historical roots to the Social Gospel Movement.

The document saw faith not as a separate list of things to accomplish, but as part of *civic muscle*, necessary for the other facets of the vision to come to life. It saw Spirit *amid* the work, not off on the side.

When you look at the outline of the other sixteen civic domains mentioned in the document, it is hard not to notice that they overlap perfectly with the creative domains of a century in the progressive era. They include housing, creative financial institutions, new forms of workforce training and ownership, social entrepreneurship and, of course, a vast complexity of public health and healthcare.

This book of prayers is not about that particular to-do list, as the specific list of possibilities constantly changes. It is about the energy and power that makes the work possible.

Prayer and Possibility

It is possible that the lowest form of both Spirit and intellect is writing about prayer. One just has no idea what any of the words mean until you can see how they are expressed in social form. For humans, jaguars, whales and eagles the highest integration of body, spirit and mind is social. For those of the YHWH camp, you look at The People and how they live together. We can look to the neighborhood to see what one's prayers produce in mercy, justice and loving kindness.

The voice of Spirit—prayer—is tested in what happens in the social body. I and other have written many pages about how faith makes possible all sorts of healing at social scale. But I don't think we've quite made the point strongly enough about how the Spirit drives the innovation: the connection between prayer and possibility. That's what this last little section is about.

I—and, I think it is fair to say, Jesus and every other mature spiritual leader—am less interested in the *spiritual* than what comes next. That is because there is no spiritual phase that does not flow immediately and surely back into the social world of others. If that doesn't happen, the phase called spiritual died in the womb.

I notice that those who tend the Spirit often find themselves drawn in a tender way into the lives of others. This tenderness is not just as simplistic as feeling badly about the differences in life circumstances such as poverty, violation and illness, although those are never overlooked. The tenderness is not only for others, but includes, weirdly, a tenderness for one's self.

I am not likely to become a great deal more grown-up in the Spirit before I run out years. But in the same way this kind of intentional vulnerability to the world and spirit makes one tender toward others, I am surprised that it makes me a bit more tender towards me, too. The flow is not just away from me, drawn out and apart from my self-consumption with my little tasks and holdings. It draws away the toxins as it draws away things of value to others, the bits of time and money and attention that one might describe as "from" me.

Even my primitive and random acts of conscious prayer do not feel like lancing a boil of selfishness at all. Rather, it feels more like a release that joins, that creates new relationship that oddly flows like a connecting thread entangling me in others' lives.

The tenderness draws *stuff* out of my life—bit of coin, time and bother, such as the mundane tasks of democracy or church. Life uses that *stuff* to draw me into relationship and resonance. I think that's what Jesus experienced in the wilderness and why he could heal so freely when he came back to the crowds. And why he urged us not to pray in public as some kind of performance.

The prayers that flow through us come up out of the life that flows through us. It is surprising this needs any other comment except to say this is the way life works. But it feels new and surprising almost every time it happens, as if we only know it by pausing to tend to the consciousness of the way life works in us and through us.

Life is the thing that works. And this is how it works—we are drawn into conscious relationships marked by practicalities and in the same moment by sanctity. *Homo sapiens sanctus.*

The *sanctus* makes the *sapiens* part smarter. The Spirit triggers a more complex consciousness tuned to the mesh of possibilities. In every beginning is an image, not just a Big Bang.

Time and again, I have seen radical and nuanced tenderness expressed in generosity with the neighbors needing a lot of *stuff* we can list as units of food, housing, transportation, cash for power and light. The FaithHealth Division in my hospital rarely says no. We find a way, usually through incredibly complex relationships inside and all around the medical complex.

These relationships are not bounded by the intricacy of rules, although we do generally follow most of the formal rules, sort of. What makes it work—when it works—is the Spirit that creates the tenderness that opens our hearts to what is actually going on in the human life draw into our presence. The intelligence, ingenuity, clever operational canniness, comes *from* that tenderness. If one has not been marinated in prayerful consciousness and drawn into consciousness of the human complexity in even one "case" of someone needing some "thing," one is not likely to be smart enough to be relevant.

Sometimes I find myself standing in the hall after some meeting and notice one of the chaplains in kindly presence with someone who has come to FaithHealth for help. In most hospitals, one calls for the chaplain when a patient has run out of days and is approaching their end, which is when Spirit is supposed to be most relevant. It is, of course. But it is just as relevant in opening up possibilities for those who are not dead, but trapped in a vortex of hurt and disarray that transcends the rational toolkit of clinical staff.

We have practices, too, of course. And we have a very thick web of partners and friends who share our spirit of tenderness. It is the tenderness that opens up a canniness about what might be yet possible for the person, their family and their life. Harder, actually, then providing comfort at the end of life.

The intelligence that comes from *sanctus* works at neighborhood levels even better, which you'd expect me to say given my social gospel heritage. This complex intelligence has very practical implications today as then. We notice that in the neighborhoods where this pattern of practical healing happens the most that the cost of care for the hospital goes down, not up.

This is what we call "proactive mercy." It is so basic and obvious that it shouldn't even be considered smart; just not dumb. When people get the *stuff,* and the *relationship* they actually need when they need it, they are less likely to require more expensive stuff, such as an emergency room for more acute medical care. More care at the right time means less care needed at a more expensive time.

Computers can predict who might need different kinds of care at optimal times. But those programs are usually confined to patients who are already pretty far down the acuity spiral with needs that are not really subtle enough to require computers.

The time when sensitivity—let's call it tenderness—provides an actual return on investment is *earlier* in the distress, when a bit of *proactive mercy* might actually help. The intelligence about how and when and with whom to be proactive in that manner comes from an alert—conscious—web of *Homo sapiens sanctus* type people with qualities of tender consciousness to pay attention and act appropriately.

If one wants efficient human communities with optimal services provided at the right time and cheapest possible cost, you just have to nurture the kind of tender spirituality that will generate the consciousness and energy to accomplish mercy at the moment it can help. If we want to heal the neighborhood, city, state, nation, hemisphere or globe, then we must pray to be tender, humble, conscious and connected enough to know what to do.

That's how the Spirit makes us available to what might be possible. That kind of prayer expresses, as courage and action, enough to save a forest plot threatened by a developer, heal a neighborhood, carry a family over a troubled water.

That's why Walter wrote his book of prayers and, a hundred years later, why I have, too.

Spirit of this sort flows when we dare to open ourselves to the first rivulets of faith that propel the first minor fruits of mercy and justice.

And then they grow a little bit more as first fruit of spirit is curiosity with the second, courage, right behind.

Spirit in the world moving us even further into the ever-surprising, ever-emerging world.

Life

One of the curious and defining obsessions of the past century has been how much of our collective energy has been organized around problems, threats and pathologies. This is powerful in some ways; we've solved a lot of problems. But it has encouraged a spirit as obsessed with the negative as any Geneva Calvinist, inquisition, or homophobic zealot was about sin.

Those of us trained into some kind of professional job are the most likely to be trapped, our identities based on the type of problem we are supposed to be able of solving. This is part of why the social gospel prayers and spirit seem so quaint and simple. The Good News was simpler because the bad news was less highly developed. A hundred years later our negative imagination has flourished to absurd levels, taking our spiritual imagination with it.

There is another way, the way of life. It is in all sorts of places where you'd not expect it, such as in the writing of Paul while he was in jail. If you're looking for sin, this is a good place to find it. But you'll find something surprising when he speaks about prayer, which I had even read in the Greek but missed the point entirely.

The passage is about prayer, not about instructions. He says the whole galaxy is already praying for us. It is *groaning* as if in childbirth. I have sisters, daughters, a wife and many women colleagues who know a lot more about the groaning of childbirth than Paul. The one thing they know that even a *man* should know, is that the groans are for life. These are not groans of lament, but expectation.

We don't even need to pray at all; not one syllable. The universe is already moving underneath and through us like a primal muscular wave propelling us toward life. That pressure you feel is your Mother-God's pelvic rippling, moving us toward life. Of course, we don't have words for that. Not even a groan for that! We're the ones being born.

We don't need to get anything right about prayer and it happens anyway.

We don't need to get the name correct, in Aramaic or Greek, Spanish or English.

No need to bow, pray with candles, or in any particular cadence.

Prayer is the absence of religion, the absolute liberation from any of its manipulative trappings.

From time to time, that groaning finds its way into the clumsy vocabulary of English. Even in English we can say words of prayer that, blunt as they are, help us tune into what is going on. As long as we don't think the *words* are the prayer, the flow of the living Spirit may still move.

The surest fruit of prayer is the end of artful religious performance. The Spirit carries us away from the altar just as Ezekiel pictured it in his wild vision of the river of life. A trickle in the sanctuary, he saw the Spirit finding its moist way under and through the religious wall. It was ankle deep as it hit the city street. Then deeper still with every step away and into the world God loves into being. With the sanctuary out of sight, now waist deep and hard to hold balance. Then a neck deep and rising. "Human, do You see it?"

I like that the prophet had to ask, maybe taunting, as we are so reluctant to see the most obvious abundance. We construct religion to hold our little protective ideas. Spirit invites into the deep water flowing fast and lively. Do You see that? The Spirit is life and liberation everywhere flowing with uncontrollable generosity that feeds the life of all it waters. That's how the world works in the reign of the Spirit. Amen.

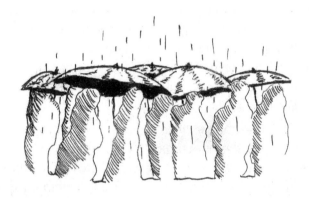

Not Anonymous

I grew up in a kind of suburban Protestant tradition where prayer was like a chat with a neighbor who just happened to create the universe. The Dalai Lama once visited Memphis and found himself receiving a fist bump from a city council member that grew up like me. The councilman also joked, "Hello Dalai!" The Dalai Lama is, technically, God, but with a sense of humor, so he grinned and bumped back. Some reading the prayers in this book will be as uncomfortable that one might speak of the Ultimate as if it could be addressed at all.

These prayers are aiming at a more respectful relationship with the Ultimate, but not less intimate. To pray as if we were not intimately related to our world is another flavor of creepy. The universe is relational in every possible aspect and scale. It is more like a home than a machine, of which we are part.

All of the sciences are ways of describing what is at root a radically relational phenomenon. Whether it is an interplay among chemicals, particles or fields of energy, the whole thing—all the way as far as we can peer into billions of light years of space—is in relation to everything else. It does echo, as one might describe music, but it's closer to say "resonate." It seems ridiculous to *describe it* as an "it." We are *related*.

We relate—not *just think*—so we are. I could have typed, "*I* am related, therefore *I* am." This is exactly where Descartes lost the plot, clever as he was. There is no "*I*" thinking little things called thoughts apart from anything. My skin does not wrap a thing called "me." By weight and function the largest part of "me" is composed of trillions of microbial forms of life. There is no "me" unrelated, apart, thinking things called "thoughts." There is no individualistic me offering things called "prayers" crossing my lips. We are related so intimately that it would be foolish not to use relational language. Speaking of "it" as if it was an unrelated "it" is just as silly as giving the Ultimate a fist bump.

The vastly intricate phenomenon in which we find ourselves alive is itself more like life and less like a machine. It moves and has a being. We are closer to being accurate with relational language than mechanical terms.

I and other friends have written about the *Leading Causes of Life* to counter the obsession with the leading causes of death. We want to balance the pathology-oriented profess-ional language that leads us away from the most interesting parts of being human—the ones that adapt, thrive and live. Life is more interesting than death. And working with life helps us be more deeply accountable for living lives about life.

The Leading Causes of Life also invites us to relate to the larger phenomenon as having qualities of life. The universe, neighborhood and family are not dead; not an "it." Not exactly a "her" or "him", buddy, "ghost" or "pixie." Alive.

In using life language, we are not *projecting* human life onto a non-human mechanical phenomenon. We humans are alive, too. *And we are not apart.*

We are small and the phenomena big. We cannot help but speaking, painting on cave walls, offering up symbolic gestures, pausing humbled. Sometimes, per-haps at the bot-tom of the Grand Canyon, we are muted in awe and gratitude to be present and related.

Something like a prayer escapes our lips. You and I are officially called Homo sapiens *sapiens*. We are conscious of being conscious. But I think there is more.

Call it a prayer. *Homo Sapiens Sanctus.*

Jesus

I'll understand if you find it uncomfortable and unseemly to move from universal phenomenon to the strange carpenter-teacher who lived two millennia ago. Long before germ theory, telescopes or electricity, Jesus lived a short life before dying as a political criminal. We know about his his life through scraps of stories and vignettes no longer alive to us except through translations of translations.

Jesus was not a member of any Christian religion and would probably not recognize most of it. Although a student of the Jewish texts, he was not a writer of any kind. No home, much less an office. No wife, apparently, or kids. We don't know his sexuality. He apparently had a brother. He healed people seven days a week with no business model. The only times he showed up at worship, he got thrown out. He never voted or sought political power. But he was regarded by Empire and its religious toadies as a threat to order. He had no school, but did accumulate disciples. Before his movement backslid into bishops, those following him were said to follow his "Way."

That's the clue. I want to move through life in that "way" and with those on that way.

He prayed some, mostly by himself, apparently to strengthen his capacity to stay on the Way.

He said that way was narrow and difficult, which some think means we should go single file through life.

I think it means we are to walk like the Caribou who move through impossibly difficult circumstances following many paths that weave together and then apart and together again. I have walked on narrow braided Caribou paths on the tundra shelves flanking the frozen Alaska rivers beneath the

Brooks Range. The Caribou have a Way that they have followed for thousands of years, moving as a company of thousands trusting each other to find the paths across and through to where the Spirit of life draws them.

The early Mediterranean Christians thought of Jesus as the lamb of God, stressing the sacrificial metaphor. They didn't know anything about Caribou and how the herd saves each other.

The mesh of trails suggests a social complexity beyond our simplistic theory of networks.[4] This helps me imagine the adaptive possibilities as Spirit sets us free while remaining social, safe while remaining kind.

I, too, pay attention to my trusted ones: Chris and Bobby, Enrique and Maria, TC, Jim, Tom, Fred, Jeremy, Jerry, Dora, Ron and a cloud of witnesses on the move. We trust each other to stay on the journey and in sight, sometimes protecting, sometimes finding safety. The world is a dangerous place. Safety only in motion, together, on the Way.

I wonder what Jesus would say about all this. I suspect he'd wonder about all the churches from which I was *not* thrown out. And all the clutter I've accumulated beyond his one cloak and borrowed mule. My offices. All the stuff I did not give away. All the healing kindnesses left for other obligations.

I hope for grace.

And pray for a Spirit to move me onto one of those narrow paths closer to the edge of the herd as we move together over tough land for another season of life.

Endnotes

1. Matthew 7:9-13.
2. Prayer of St. Francis, traditionally attributed to St. Francis of Assisi, though it does not appear in any of his writings.
3. Reinhold Niebuhr offered various versions of the Serenity Prayer in his sermons, beginning in 1934. The prayer opens with the familiar words: "God grant me the serenity to accept the things I cannot change; courage to change the things I can; and wisdom to know the difference."
4. Ingold, Tim. The life of lines. Oxon & New York: Routledge; 2015.